The Fox

Playful Prowler

text by Christian Havard

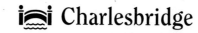 Charlesbridge

Library of Congress Cataloging-in-Publication Data
Havard, Christian.
    [Renard, rôdeur solitaire. English]
    The fox, playful prowler / text by Christian Havard; photography
by Jacana; French series editor Valérie Tracqui.
        p.   cm. – (Animal close-ups)
    ISBN 0-88106-434-3 (softcover)
    1. Foxes–Behavior–Juvenile literature.   2. Foxes–Juvenile literature.
[1. Foxes.] I. Jacana, Viäl, ill.   II. Title.   III. Series.
QL737.C22H38 1995   94-22172
599.74'442–dc20   CIP
                                                                      AC

Copyright © Éditions Milan 1992.
300 rue Léon-Joulin 31101 Toulouse, France.
Original edition first published by Éditions Milan under the title *Le renard, rôdeur solitaire.*
French series editor, Valérie Tracqui

The fox is related to the dog and has many of the same kinds of behaviors such as panting when hot and burying food.

The little (13 pound), shy fox is nothing like the big, bad wolf.

A few blackberries are a delicious dessert.

The quick red fox jumps over the lazy brown dog

It is autumn. Red and gold leaves flutter gracefully down to the wet, fragrant soil. A new day begins with a concert of singing blackbirds, robins, and warblers. An owl flies back to its daytime sleeping hollow.

The fox has a full belly and is ready to go to sleep. It runs around in a circle like a dog to find a good spot to lie down. It sleeps all day under a blackberry bush, where it is protected from the wind and out of sight.

A-hunting we will go

At sundown, the fox wakes up and goes off to hunt. Criss-crossing back and forth through its territory, the fox sniffs and listens.

Now the fox stops, ears twitching. It hears and smells a tiny mouse 150 feet away. The mouse does not suspect anything. It is eating the seeds of grasses growing along the water's edge. Mouse sounds and scent lead the fox toward the pond.

With tail straight out behind it and ears down, the fox creeps forward silently. Closer and closer it comes until, all of a sudden, it leaps up and pounces on the mouse. The mouse was tasty, perhaps, but the fox is still hungry. It needs about a pound of food a day. That means several more mice or . . . something bigger.

The fox uses all its senses, especially smell and hearing, to stalk and capture its prey.

Gotcha! The fox leaps up and pounces on its prey.

6

While climbing on the rocks, this fox found a dead sea gull to eat.

Foxes are surprisingly good climbers. This fox is looking for eggs to eat.

Foxes hunt well at night because they have keen eyesight. Their eye pupils open wide in dim light and close into narrow slits in bright light just like the eyes of a cat.

What's for supper?

The fox has caught a duck. It took several hours of smelling scents, tracking sounds, sneaking up, and pouncing before the fox could get this food. Most days the food is a rabbit or some mouse-like voles, but birds, eggs, insects, roots, fruits, berries, frogs, and fish are also on the menu. If it is hungry, a fox will eat dead animals or garbage.

The fox doesn't hunt for sport. Food is its goal, and usually the slowest, sickest, or oldest prey becomes its supper. If there is too much to eat at one meal, the fox may cover the leftovers with earth, leaves, or snow to save them for another day.

A healthy, fast, and careful bird, mouse, or rabbit is not easy to catch.

Strangers in the night

In the beginning of January, it is time for the lonely male to find a mate. He forgets about hunting all the time and runs for miles each night looking for a female.

The female, called a vixen, is also out looking. She leaves tracks and scent messages for the male.

Usually quiet, the foxes now call out to each other, barking to signal where they are. Yap-yap-yap-yaaaa!

When the male and female find each other, they sniff, roll over, and frolic in the grass.

They will share the work of raising their family.

Playful nipping is just one of the ways the male and female get to know each other before mating.

The pair will share their food and prepare a den
for their babies, which are called kits or pups.

Foxes are protected from the cold by thick winter coats of fur. Because foxes weigh only eight to sixteen pounds, they can walk on the snow without sinking far down into it.

All is calm, all is white

It's winter. New snow has fallen, making the countryside white and silent. In the den, the vixen is busy. She cleans and digs out a bigger space so that her babies will be comfortable. The den had been a rabbit hole, so it will take some work to prepare it.

The male spends his nights out hunting again. The tracks of prey are easy to spot in the snow, but there are few to find. The voles are crouched underground, and the rabbits are hidden under the blackberry bushes. A partridge, numb from the cold, is a welcome meal for the male to catch and share with the vixen.

Where the wild foxes are

It will soon be the end of winter. As is his habit, the fox regularly marks the boundaries of his territory. In each place, he leaves several drops of urine and scent from special scent glands near his tail and on his hind feet.

These two cousins cannot be sure whose territory they are on. Watch out for the sharp teeth!

The foxes mark their territory so that other foxes will leave and find another place to live.

One of the fastest mammals in North America, the red fox can gallop as fast as 45 miles per hour!

On wet ground or sand, the tracks of a fox are easy to recognize.

The fox warns other animals that this is his territory. When territories overlap or are shared by several creatures, each one knows the smell of the others. An animal with an unfamiliar smell is in for trouble! The fox snarls at strangers, showing off his big, sharp teeth and growling fiercely. A stranger is likely to leave with some bites and a torn ear.

Peek-a-boo,
I see you!

It is mid-March and the daffodils are blooming, but the vixen hasn't left her den in four days. The father-to-be waits outside in the warm sun.

Finally, five little fox pups are born. They are 6 inches long with $2\frac{1}{2}$ inch tails. Their silky skin is almost black and is covered with a fuzzy coat of brownish fur. Their blue eyes will not open for over a week.

By playing games, each day the fox pups become faster and smarter.

Curious about everything, a one-month-old fox pup looks around outside the den for the first time.

Now that they are six weeks old, the mother feeds them outside the den. They have to hurry because she is in a rush to go out hunting.

At eight weeks old, the pups eyes change color from blue to golden brown.

The pups have their first outing when they are 5 weeks old. What a big day! They roll in the wet grass, running after the first butterflies, biting, leaping, and tumbling. Their mother needs to remind them not to wander off too far.

The happy pups hold their tails straight up. When puzzled, they tip their heads to one side and lower their tails. When they are frightened by a strange sound, they run back into the den with their ears back and tails down.

Waiting for their parents to come back, the pups stay in the den.

Outside the den, the pups feel safe only if their parents are close by. The pups learn to listen carefully to the noises they hear outside.

Cricket anyone?

The pups are now eight weeks old. Their fur is beginning to turn red, and they are learning to hunt. One pup chases and catches a cricket! The pup trots around with the cricket in its mouth as the other pups follow curiously.

Several times a day the mother or father brings them food. When the father comes back with a field mouse, the pups all grab it and play tug of war until each one has only a small piece. After eating, the pups play.

They climb all over their mother and practice pouncing on the white tip of her wagging tail. One pup finds a stick to chew and carry around. This is a prize worth fighting over!

By the fifth week, the mother feeds meat to the babies.

Watch out for new discoveries, not everything is safe to eat.

Look, up in the sky!

By mid-summer, the pups have lost their baby teeth, and permanent teeth have grown in. Each night, they follow their parents farther and farther from the den and sleep out in the fields. The pups know about danger, but they often forget to be careful.

Larger animals such as bear, wolf, and mountain lion sometimes kill foxes, but do not usually bother with them. Eagles and great horned owls, however, eat fox pups whenever they can!

One early autumn morning, an eagle spots one of the pups and dives toward it without a sound. Luckily, the pup sees the bird's shadow and runs between two rocks. The life of a fox is very dangerous. . . .

The lynx and the bobcat will kill any foxes they find.

A tired pup falls asleep in the sun unaware of any danger.

The biggest danger comes from the sky. The eagle attacks fox pups and the weakest adults.

Curiosity and the ability to learn will help this pup survive.

Little fox in the big woods

In late August, the fox family splits up. It's time for the foxes to separate because the territory will not have enough prey animals to feed them all. Like most hunting animals, the fox does not store food to last during the winter. It goes out to hunt every day and may cross 10 square miles in winter if food is scarce.

A fox can see motion but not shape, so a smart rabbit stays still. The pups have learned to face into the wind while rabbit hunting so that they can pick up the scent. In fact, the pups have learned their lessons so well that, come January, each one will be big enough to look for a mate and start a new fox family!

These pups will have a life full of adventures when they leave the family at the end of the summer.

The fox

Many people admire the fox for its beautiful fur, independence, and cleverness. Many other people dislike the fox because it steals chickens from farms. Some people fear the fox because they confuse it with the coyote and the wolf.

Hunted
People have hunted the fox with guns, poison, and traps. To help protect the fox population, some states limit the length of the hunting season and the types of traps that can be used.

In England, where fox hunting is considered the sport of kings, people treat the fox with respect. They hunt the fox by chasing it to its den with the help of special dogs. These hunters do not hurt the fox. In other parts of the world, a fox hunt ends with the death of the fox.

In the olden days, hunters and trappers were paid a bounty for killing a fox.

What beautiful fur!
The fox has long been hunted for its very long and thick fur. Today, many clothes designers refuse to use fur; others will only use fur that comes from animals raised on special fur farms. Very few fox furs come from wild animals.

For a long time, thousands of fox skins were bought to make fur coats.

What kind of future?

Many scientific studies show that the fox is a very important part of the food chain. Foxes eat mice, voles, and other rodents. Without foxes, these rodents would have a population explosion.

To kill all the foxes, raccoons, skunks, and other wild animals in order to stop the spread of rabies would be horrible. It is a law that all dogs must have rabies shots. Scientists have been trying to protect wild animals, too, by putting the rabies vaccine in food that they leave out where wild animals will eat it.

The main obstacle to the survival of foxes is that people now live and work on much of the land where foxes used to live. Less land means that young foxes cannot find a territory of their own. Some foxes live in suburban woods, where they compete with raccoons and skunks for the limited food.

Towns and suburbs tempt the fox with their garbage.

Some people keep foxes as pets, but wild animals can never be totally tamed.

	FOX	**COYOTE**	**WOLF**
weight	10-16 lbs.	25-40 lbs.	45-100+ lbs.
ears	large, pointed	large, pointed	short, rounded
nose	narrow, pointed	pointed	heavier, dog-like
tail	held high when running	held low when running	held high when running
diet	mice, rabbits, voles, insects, berries, birds, squirrel	rabbits, mice, insects, squirrels, carrion, reptiles, prairie dog	caribou, moose, sheep, squirrel, mice, marmot, carrion

The family of foxes

The fox belongs to the big family of *canines*. The dog is the most well known canine, but the wolf, jackal, and coyote are also members of this family. More than twenty species of foxes live throughout the world. The red fox inhabits a greater area of the world than any other species of wild mammal!

▲
The wolf is an evil character in folktales probably because it has competed with hunting and farming people for thousands of years. Wolves were once the most widespread mammal, but they have been hunted so much that now there are refuges to protect wolves. Most wolves live and hunt in well-organized packs. The strongest male is the leader of the pack. He may weigh as much as 175 pounds.

◀ The Arctic fox has a magnificent coat of fur that changes from white in the winter to gray in the summer. Hunted for this valuable fur, it almost became extinct, but today is protected. Well adapted to the extreme cold of the Arctic, it is comfortable in temperatures as low as -50 degrees F. It weighs only about 10 pounds. It often follows polar bears and polar wolves to eat their leftovers.

◀ The coyote lives in North America from Alaska to Mexico. It weighs between 25 and 40 pounds. It eats rabbits, mice, voles, fruit, and lizards. Its larger size and long, thin legs make it also a feared predator of lambs and calves. The coyote is famous for its howl, but like most other members of the canine family, it woofs and barks, too.

The fennec fox, weighing less than 3½ pounds, is the smallest of the foxes. It is perfectly adapted to its home in the deserts of Africa and eastern Asia. It has fur on the bottom of its paws so it can walk on hot desert sands. Its thick coat of fur protects it from both cold desert nights and hot desert sun. Its big ears help it hear the slightest sounds of the lizards and insects it hunts for food.

▶